World Wisdom
The Library of Perennial Philosophy

The Library of Perennial Philosophy is dedicated to the exposition of the timeless Truth underlying the diverse religions. This Truth, often referred to as the *Sophia Perennis*—or Perennial Wisdom—finds its expression in the revealed Scriptures as well as the writings of the great sages and the artistic creations of the traditional worlds.

The Perennial Philosophy provides the intellectual principles capable of explaining both the formal contradictions and the underlying unity of the great religions.

Ranging from the writings of the great sages who have expressed the *Sophia Perennis* in the past, to the perennialist authors of our time, each series of our Library has a different focus. As a whole, they express the inner unanimity, transforming radiance, and irreplaceable values of the great spiritual traditions. *Christian Spirit* appears as one of our selections in the Sacred Worlds series.

Sacred Worlds Series

The Sacred Worlds series blends images of visual beauty with focused selections from the writings of the great religions of the world, including both Scripture and the writings of the sages and saints. Books in the Sacred Worlds series may be based upon a particular religious tradition, or a theme of interest, such as prayer and virtue, which are found in all manifestations of the sacred.

Forthcoming books by Judith and Michael Oren Fitzgerald

The Sermon of All Creation: Christians on Nature, forthcoming 2005
The Spirit of Indian Women, forthcoming 2006

Other books by Michael Oren Fitzgerald

Yellowtail, Crow Medicine Man and Sun Dance Chief, 1991
Light on the Indian World: The Essential Writings of Charles Eastman (Ohiyesa), 2002
Indian Spirit, 2003

Other World Wisdom books on Christianity

Chartres and the Birth of the Cathedral, by Titus Burckhardt, 1995
The Fullness of God: Frithjof Schuon on Christianity, edited by James S. Cutsinger, 2004
In the Heart of the Desert: The Spirituality of the Desert Fathers and Mothers, by John Chryssavgis, 2003
Not of This World: A Treasury of Christian Mysticism, edited by James S. Cutsinger, 2003
Paths to the Heart: Sufism and the Christian East, edited by James S. Cutsinger, 2002

Christian Spirit

Edited by

Judith Fitzgerald
and
Michael Oren Fitzgerald

World Wisdom

Christian Spirit
©2004 World Wisdom, Inc.

Design by Judith Fitzgerald

Library of Congress Cataloging-in-Publication Data

Christian spirit / edited by Judith Fitzgerald and Michael Oren Fitzgerald.
    p. cm. – (Sacred worlds series)
 Includes bibliographical references and index.
 ISBN 0-941532-64-X (pbk. : alk. paper)
 1. Spiritual life–Christianity. I. Fitzgerald, Judith, 1951- II. Fitzgerald, Michael Oren, 1949-
III. Title. IV. Series: Sacred worlds series (Bloomington, Ind.)

 BV4501.3.C495 2004
 270–dc22

                                                                2004009155

Cover art: Thirteenth-century illumination depicting the Heavenly Jerusalem

Printed on acid-free paper in China.

For information address World Wisdom, Inc.
P.O. Box 2682, Bloomington, Indiana 47402-2682

www.worldwisdom.com

Table of Contents

small thing is not small when it leads to something great; and it is no small matter to forsake the ancient tradition of the Church that was upheld by all those who were called before us, whose conduct we should observe, and whose faith we should imitate.

John of Damascus (675-749)

Introduction

For over two millennia Christianity has been the central source of spiritual inspiration for billions of people all around the globe. Although the West is increasingly becoming characterized by a religious pluralism, Christianity continues to be its predominant religion. Readers have access to the words of Christ and his Apostles, and bookstores in the West contain an abundance of material from more recent centuries on Christian thought in each of the branches of Christianity.[1] But the words of the Christian saints and sages before the time of the Reformation are not as readily available. Thus, the goal of this book is to provide a taste of both the spiritual wisdom and sacred art of Christianity during approximately the first one and a half millennia of its existence, beginning with the period immediately after the twelve Apostles.

✛ ✛ ✛

One intention is to emphasize the unity that exists within all Christian spirituality. We have, therefore, organized the book in a more or less chronological order, instead of strictly separating the materials to reflect the different Christian denominations. We believe that the reader will easily move between the words and sacred art from these different sources without finding any inherent contradictions. We hope a deeper understanding of this common spiritual bond will bring Christians closer together. In a similar manner, by

---

[1] When we speak of the different branches of Christianity we have in mind the various Eastern Orthodox Churches, Roman Catholicism, and Protestantism.

introducing believers of other faiths to these masterpieces of sacred art and texts of Christian wisdom, we hope they will develop a deeper appreciation of the early Christian spirit.

✠ ✠ ✠

For Christians, Christ is the manifestation of the Divine Logos—the Divine Truth on earth and "the Light of the world."[2] This luminous Truth continued to shine through the writings of great Christian sages and sacred artistic creations, which form a central part of the Christian spiritual tradition. This time-honored tradition, built over centuries, helps provide a guiding light to spiritual seekers because it refers us back to the Divine Truth that is the ultimate source of the religion.[3] In today's world many people seek happiness by cultivating lifestyles based on egoism and materialism and they fail to recognize that it is only through conformation to objective principles of truth and beauty that the human soul can discover the deep springs of joy from which all forms of happiness arise. The importance of turning to the great religions to find the spiritual light to purify and illuminate our actions cannot be over-emphasized. It is also increasingly difficult for those who acknowledge the existence of spiritual principles to remember them during the daily turmoil of our fast-paced society. We hope this book will become a daily inspirational companion to facilitate that remembrance.

✠ ✠ ✠

---

[2] The form of the central manifestation of the Logos may vary in each religion. In Buddhism, the Buddha is also a human manifestation of the Divine Logos; however, in Judaism and Islam, the Logos descended in the form of the Torah and the Koran.

[3] We note that the word "religion" is based upon the Latin word *religio*, "to bind back," thus meaning all that binds man back to God.

Another goal of this book is to present works of art that embody the spiritual vision of Christianity in both depth and breadth. But is there such a concept as "sacred art" and, if so, why is it important? Let us quote Titus Burckhardt on the principles of sacred art:

> No art merits the epithet sacred unless its very forms reflect the spiritual vision characteristic of a particular religion. Every form "vehicles" a particular quality of being. The religious subject of a work of art can be merely superimposed on a form, in which case it lacks any relation to the formal "language" of the work, as is demonstrated by Christian art since the Renaissance. Such productions are merely profane works of art with a religious theme....
>
> Every sacred art is therefore founded on a science of forms, or in other words, on the symbolism inherent in forms. It must be borne in mind that a sacred symbol is not merely a conventional sign; it manifests its archetype by virtue of a certain ontological law....
>
> The ultimate objective of sacred art is not to evoke feelings or communicate impressions; it is a symbol, and as such it employs simple and primordial means. It cannot in any case be anything more than allusive, its real object being ineffable.[4]

Frithjof Schuon provides us with specific guidance concerning Christian art, which correctly defines most of the artwork in *Christian Spirit*:

> Christian art comprises essentially three images: the Virgin and Child, the Crucifixion, the Holy Visage: the first image relates to

---

[4] Titus Burckhardt, *The Essential Titus Burckhardt: Reflections on Sacred Art, Faiths, and Civilizations*, ed. William Stoddart (Bloomington, IN: World Wisdom, 2003), p. 87. Titus Burckhardt, a German Swiss, was born in Florence in 1908 and died in Lausanne in 1984. A prolific author, he devoted all his life to the study and exposition of the different aspects of Wisdom and Tradition.

the Incarnation, the second to the Redemption and the third to the Divinity of Christ. Man recapitulates these three symbols or mysteries respectively by purity which is the vehicle of "Christ in us," by death to the world, and by sanctity or wisdom.[5]

For the contemplative soul, beauty possesses an alchemical quality which melts hardness of heart and removes psychic obstacles from the mind; it creates an atmosphere of recollection that allows for the remembrance of God and it may thus serve as a partial remedy to antidote the ugliness in the modern world.

✛ ✛ ✛

In today's technological world we often lose our connection with anything of sacred value that can provide a balance for the disequilibriating factors that we encounter on a daily basis. It is our hope that the insights provided in *Christian Spirit*, both through the words of these great sages and through sacred art from over a millennium of Christianity, will help each of us to better understand the sacred spirit that dwells within every person.

Judith and Michael Fitzgerald
March, 2004
Bloomington, Indiana

---

[5] Frithjof Schuon, *Gnosis: Divine Wisdom* (Bedfont, Middlesex: Perennial Books, 1990), p. 107. Frithjof Schuon was born in 1907 in Basle, Switzerland, of German parents and died in the United States in 1998. Schuon is best known as the foremost spokesman of the Perennial Philosophy and as a philosopher in the metaphysical current of Shankara and Plato.

Page from the Lindisfarne Gospels, Celtic

Man is made for the contemplation of heaven, and is in truth a heavenly plant, intended to come to the knowledge of God.

Clement of Alexandria (150-220)

hat you may be able to know God, first know yourself.

Cyprian of Carthage (d. 258)

he Creator of the world is the Word of God: and this is our Lord, who was made man, existing in this world, and who in an invisible manner contains all things created, and is inherent in the entire creation, since the Word of God governs and arranges all things; and therefore He came to His own in a visible manner, and was made flesh, and hung upon a tree, that He might sum up all things in Himself.

Irenaeus of Lyons (129-203)

od, being eternally good and bounteous, gave man power over good and evil. He made him the gift of spiritual knowledge so that, through contemplating the world and what is in it, he might come to know Him who created all things for man's sake. But the impious are free to choose not to know. They are free to disbelieve, to make mistakes and to conceive ideas which are contrary to the truth. Such is the degree to which man has power over good and evil.

Anthony the Great (251-356)

Monastery of St. George, Wadi el-Kelt
desert of Judaea

Anthony the Great

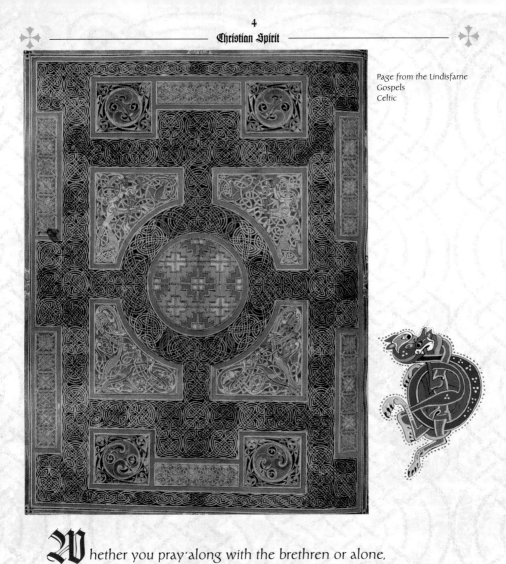

Page from the Lindisfarne
Gospels
Celtic

W hether you pray along with the brethren or alone,
strive to make your prayer more than a mere habit.
Make it a true inner experience.

Evagrius of Pontus (512-582)

hen Saint Patrick was sent to Ireland, he was confronted by a Druidic society headed by kings and tribal chieftains. In reply to a question from a Druid's daughter about the nature of the Christian God, Patrick said, "Our God is the God of all men, the God of Heaven and Earth, of sea and river, of sun and moon and stars, of the lofty mountain and the lowly valley, the God above Heaven, the God in Heaven, the God under Heaven. He has His dwelling round Heaven and Earth and the sea and all that is in them. He inspires all, He quickens all, He rules over all, He sustains all. He lights the light of the sun; He furnishes the light of the light; He has put springs in the dry land and has set stars to minister to the greater lights...."

Patrick of Ireland (385-471)

ow among spiritual gifts there is one that is indeed the greatest of them all, namely that word of knowledge which is imparted by the Holy Spirit (1 Cor. 12:8).... The supreme function of knowledge is, therefore, to know the Trinity; and, in the second place, to know God's creation, even as did he who said, For He hath given me the true knowledge of the things that are....

Origen (185-254)

Let us consider that we are standing in God's sight. We must please the divine eyes with the posture of our body as well as the measure of our voice.

Cyprian of Carthage (d. 258)

How preposterous and absurd it is, that while we ask that the will of God should be done, yet when God calls and summons us from this world, we should not at once obey the command of His will! We struggle and resist, and like obstinate servants we are dragged into the presence of the Lord with sadness and grief, departing from this world only under the bondage of necessity and not with the obedience of a free will; and yet we wish to be honored with heavenly rewards by the One to whom we come so unwillingly!

Cyprian of Carthage (d. 258)

We don't say "My Father, who art in heaven," nor "Give me this day my daily bread"; nor does each one ask that only his own debt should be forgiven him; nor does he request for himself alone that he may not be led into temptation and may be delivered from evil. Our prayer is public and common; and when we pray, we pray not for one, but for the whole people, because we the whole people are one.

Cyprian of Carthage (d. 258)

ΑΠΟϹ ΚΟΛΛΟΥΘΟϹ   ΘΕΙ ϹΙΑ   ΟΓΙΑ   ΜΑΡΙΑ

Mural in Anthony the Great's Tomb
Abyssinian

eath is not an ending, but a transition, and — this
journey through time having been completed — a
passage into eternity. Who would not hasten
to better things?

Cyprian of Carthage (d. 258)

Now let us seal the whole argument with a brief summarization. The world was made for this reason, that we might be born. We, in turn, are born, that we might know God, the Maker of the world and of us. We know, in turn, that we may worship. And again, we worship so that we may receive immortality as the reward of our labors—for the worship of God entails great labors indeed. And, in turn, we are recompensed with the reward of immortality so that, having been made like the angels, we may serve the Most High Father and Lord forever and may be an everlasting kingdom unto God.

Lactantius (252-317)

But he who carries his riches in his soul, and instead of God's Spirit bears in his heart gold or land, and is always acquiring possessions without end, and is perpetually on the outlook for more, bending downwards and fettered in the toils of the world, whence can he be able to desire and to mind the Kingdom of Heaven—a man who carries not a heart, but land or metal, who must perforce be found in the midst of the objects he has chosen? For where the mind of man is, there is also his treasure.

Clement of Alexandria (150-220)

easts bear witness to the faith ... (but) in truth the most difficult of sciences is to know one's self. Not only our eye, from which nothing outside us escapes, cannot see itself, but our mind, so piercing to discover the sins of others, is slow to recognize its own faults. Thus my speech, after eagerly investigating what is external to myself, is slow and hesitating in exploring my own nature. Yet the beholding of heaven and earth does not make us know God better than the attentive study of our being does. I am, says the Prophet (Psalm 139:14), fearfully and wonderfully made; that is to say, in observing myself I have known Thy infinite wisdom.

Basil the Great (329-379)

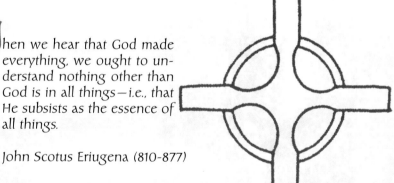

hen we hear that God made everything, we ought to understand nothing other than God is in all things—i.e., that He subsists as the essence of all things.

John Scotus Eriugena (810-877)

ot everything that can be done ought to be done.... If you think that God gave you riches for the sole purpose of enjoying them thoroughly yourself—without using them for the purposes of salvation—then you're sinning against God. For God gave us a voice, too, but that doesn't mean we must use it to sing indecent love songs. And God willed that iron be mined from the earth, but not so that we would murder one another with weapons crafted from it.

Cyprian of Carthage (d. 258)

Woman has the same spiritual dignity as man. Both of them have the same God, the same Teacher, the same Church. They breathe, see, hear, hope and love in the same way. Beings who have the same life, grace and salvation are called ... to the same manner of being.

Clement of Alexandria (150-220)

The Virgin
Abyssinian

The fact of being created in the image of God means that humanity, right from the moment of creation, was endowed with a royal character.... The Godhead is Wisdom and Logos; in yourself too you see intelligence and thought, images of the original intelligence and thought.... God is love and source of love: the divine Creator has drawn this feature on our faces too.

Gregory of Nyssa (330-395)

He who created human beings in order to make them share in His own fullness so disposed their nature that it contains the principle of all that is good, and each of these dispositions draws them to desire the corresponding divine attribute. So God could not have deprived them of the best and most precious of His attributes: self-determination, freedom.

Gregory of Nyssa (330-395)

True perfection consists in having but one fear: the fear of losing God's friendship.

Gregory of Nyssa (330-395)

St. George
Abyssinian

The man who has sharp vision for God alone is blind in all the other things that attract the eyes of the multitude.... Sharp-eyed and clear-sighted is the man who looks only to the Good with the single eye of his soul.

Gregory of Nyssa (330-395)

Laibela Church
Abyssinian

an, it is to be noted, has community with things inanimate and participates in the life of the unreasoning creatures, and shares in the mental processes of those endowed with reason. For the bond of union between man and inanimate things is the body and its composition out of the four elements: and the bond between man and plants consists, in addition to these things, of their powers of nourishment and growth and seeding, that is, generation: and finally, over and above these links, man is connected with unreasoning animals by appetite, that is anger and desire, and sense and impulsive movement … plus the five physical senses.…

Lastly, man's reason unites him to incorporeal and intelligent natures, for he applies his reason and mind and judgment to everything and pursues after virtues and eagerly follows after piety, which is the crown of the virtues. And so man is a microcosm.

John of Damascus (675-749)

It is God Himself Who brought our race to possession of things in common, first by sharing Himself and by sending His Word to all men alike, and by making all things for all.

Therefore, everything is in common, and the rich should not grasp a greater share. The expression, "I own something and have more than enough; why should I not enjoy it?" is not worthy of man nor does it indicate any community feeling.

The alternative expression however does: "I have something, why should I not share it with those in need?" Such a one is on the right path, and fulfills the command: Thou shalt love thy neighbor as thyself.

Clement of Alexandria (150-220)

The whole life of a good Christian is a holy desire to see God as He is. Now what you long for, you do not yet see, but longing makes you capable of being filled when at last you behold what you have desired.... God, by making us wait in hope, stretches our desire; by making us desire, He stretches our soul; by stretching our soul, He makes it capable of holding more. So let us desire, brothers, for we shall be filled.

Augustine of Hippo (354-430)

Page from the Book of Kells
Celtic

The Fanlo Beatus
Spanish Romanesque

ou alone are unutterable,
   from the time You created all things that can be spoken of.
You alone are unknowable,
   from the time You created all things that can be known.
All things cry out about You;
   those which speak and those which cannot speak.
All things honor You;
   those which think, and those which cannot think.
For there is one longing, one groaning,
   that all things have for You....
All things pray to You that comprehend your plan
   and offer You a silent hymn.
In You, the One, all things abide,
   and all things endlessly run to You Who art the end of all.

Gregory Nazianzus (329-389)

he Almighty power of God
rules over all things, and in
His Name all our movements
are directed, Himself being our
governor.

Columba (521-597)

St. Anthony's Monastary, Egypt

$\mathfrak{W}$hat is the will of God for us in this world? That we should do what He has ordered, that is, that we should live in righteousness and seek devotedly those things which are eternal. How do we arrive at this? By study. We must therefore study devotedly and righteously. What is our best help in maintaining this study? The Intellect, which probes everything and, finding none of the world's goods in which it can permanently rest, is converted by reason toward the One Good which is that which is eternal.

Columba (521-597)

$\mathfrak{T}$hese are bad times," people are saying, "troublesome times!" If only our lives were all good, our times would be good, for we ourselves make our times — as we are, so are our times. But what can we do? After all, we cannot convert the mass of humanity to a good life. But let the few who do listen to the will of God live good lives; and let the few who live good lives endure the many who do not. The good are the wheat, still on the threshing floor; and though the chaff lies with them there, the chaff will not come with them to the barn.

Augustine of Hippo (354-430)

$\mathfrak{R}$eprimand and rebuke should be accepted as healing remedies for vice and as conductive to good health. From this it is clear that those who pretend to be tolerant because they wish to flatter — those who thus fail to correct sinners — actually cause them to suffer supreme loss and plot the destruction of that life which is their true life.

Basil the Great (329-379)

The contemplation of nature abates the fever of the soul, and banishes all insincerity and presumption.

Basil the Great (329-379)

You are a world within a world. Become quiet and look within yourself, and see there the whole creation. Do not look at exterior things but turn all your attention to that which lies within. Gather together your whole mind within the intellectual treasure-house of your soul, and make ready for the Lord a shrine free from images.

Nilus of Ancyra (363-430)

There is then only one God, Maker of souls and bodies; one Creator of heaven and earth, the Maker of angels and archangels.... This Father of our Lord Jesus Christ is not circumscribed in any place, nor is He less than the heavens; but the heavens are the works of His fingers, and the whole world is held in His grasp: He is in all things and around all things.

Cyril of Jerusalem (315-386)

Monastery of the Syrians, Egypt

F or he who holds possessions, and gold, and houses, as the gifts of God, and ministers from them to God who gives them for the salvation of men, and knows that he possesses them more for the sake of the brethren than his own, and is superior to the possession of them, not the slave of the things he possesses, and does not carry them about in his soul, nor bind his life within them, but is ever laboring at some good and divine work, even should he be deprived of them, this man is able with cheerful mind to bear their removal equally with their abundance. This is he who is blessed by the Lord, and a meet heir of the Kingdom of Heaven, not one who could not live rich.

Clement of Alexandria (150-220)

I f evil is neither uncreated nor created by God, from whence comes its nature? Certainly that evil exists, no one living in the world will deny. What shall we say then? Evil is not a living, animated essence; it is a condition of the soul opposed to virtue, developed in the careless on account of their falling away from good.

Basil the Great (329-379)

W e practice the virtues in order to achieve contemplation of the inner essences of created things, and from this we pass to contemplation of the Logos who gives them their being; and He manifests Himself when we are in a state of prayer.

Evagrius of Pontus (512-582)

Page from the Book of Kells
Celtic

 **S**piritual insight is characterized first by awareness of one's own failings before they issue in outward signs ... and second by the knowledge of the mysteries hidden in the divine Scriptures and in the sensible creation.

Peter of Damascus (1027-1107)

Let us not esteem worldly prosperity or adversity as if they were real things or things of any importance, but let us live elsewhere, and raise all our attention to heaven; counting sin as the only true evil, and nothing truly good but virtue, which unites us to God.

Gregory Nazianzus (329-389)

To know oneself has always been, so it seems, the greatest of all lessons. For, if anyone knows himself, he will know God; and in knowing God, he will become like Him, not by wearing golden ornaments or by trailing long flowing robes, but by performing good deeds and cultivating an independence of as many things as possible. God alone has no needs, and He rejoices in a particular way when He sees us pure in the adornment of our minds and our bodies clothed with the adornment of the holy garment of self-control.

Clement of Alexandria (150-220)

othing in creation has erred from the path of God's purpose for it, save only man. Sun, moon, stars, water, air, none of these has swerved from their order, but, knowing the Word as their Maker and their King, remained as they were made. Men alone, having rejected what is good, have invented nothings instead of the truth, and have ascribed the honor due to God and knowledge concerning Him to demons and men in the form of stones.

Athanasius (297-373)

he soul possesses freedom; and though the Devil can make suggestions, he doesn't have the power to compel you against your will.

Cyril of Jerusalem (315-386)

man might seem to confess the Lord and hear His words, yet if he does not obey the Lord's commands, he is condemned—even if, by some divine concession, he is vouchsafed an endowment of spiritual gifts.

Basil the Great (329-379)

He who is educated and eloquent must not measure his saintliness merely by his fluency. Of two imperfect things, holy rusticity is better than sinful eloquence.

Jerome (340-420)

Men go abroad to wonder at the height of mountains, at the huge waves of the sea, at the long courses of the rivers, at the vast compass of the ocean, at the circular motion of the stars—yet they pass by themselves without wondering.

Augustine of Hippo (354-430)

Suppose we were to ... draw the outline of a circle. ... Let us suppose that this circle is the world, and that God Himself is the center; the straight lines drawn from the circumference are the lives of men. ... The closer those lines are to God, the closer they become to one another; and the closer they are to one another, the closer they become to God.

Dorotheos of Gaza (500-560)

No man can use his visual sense alone and properly comprehend the greatness of the heavens, or the extent of the earth, or the order of all things. How could bodily eyes ever manage to grasp things that transcend mind and understandings? It is only with difficulty that the mind can gain a true contemplation of existing reality, and only then after it has been purified of its own opinions, freed of its prejudices, and illumined by the grace and mercy of God. Even then, it only perceives insofar as it has been illumined.

John Scotus Eriugena (810-877)

*S*acred scripture does not set men and women in opposition to one another in respect to gender. Sex does not constitute any difference in the sight of God.

Origen (185-254)

*H*ave you begun to stop trying to defend your sins? Then you have made a beginning of righteousness.

Augustine of Hippo (354-430)

Page from the Lindisfarne Gospels
Celtic

The White Monastery
Deir el-Abiad. Egypt

The Christian prays in every situation, in his walks for recreation, in his dealings with others, in silence, in reading, in all rational pursuits.

Clement of Alexandria (150-220)

All our life is like a day of celebration for us; we are convinced, in fact, that God is always everywhere. We work while singing; we sail while reciting hymns; we accomplish all other occupations of life while praying.

Clement of Alexandria (150-220)

The world is an arena and a running place ... and this (our time in this earthly life) is a time of struggle.... In order to overcome in this struggle, our attention must be constantly directed toward God: for the Lord is the Omnipotent, the Almighty, the Victorious at all times, whenever He descends into the body of mortals to fight for them. But it is manifest that those who are defeated ... are those whose will is stripped of Him because of their injustice.

Isaac the Syrian (7th century)

God does not ask for our blood, but for our faith.

Cyprian of Carthage (d. 258)

The Epiphany
Coptic Painting

There are many kinds of alms the giving of which helps us to obtain pardon for our sins; but none is of greater than that by which we forgive from our heart a sin that someone has committed against us.

Augustine of Hippo (354-430)

This is robbery not to share one's resources. Perhaps what I am saying astonishes you. Yet be not astonished. For I shall offer you the testimony of the sacred scriptures, which say that not only to rob others' property, but also not to share your own with others, is robbery and greediness and theft ... "for the robbery of the poor is in your houses" (Malachi 3:10). Because you have not made offerings, the prophet says, therefore have you robbed the things that belong to the poor. This he says by way of showing the rich that they are in possession of the property of the poor, even if it is a patrimony that they have received, even if they have gathered their money elsewhere.

John Chrysostom (347-407)

Humility is the foundation of all the other virtues: hence, in the soul in which this virtue does not exist there cannot be any other virtue except in mere appearance.

Augustine of Hippo (354-430)

The man to whom a little is not enough, he will not benefit from more. He who tramples upon the world, tramples upon himself.

Columbanus (543-615)

I saw all the devil's traps set upon the earth, and I groaned and said, "Who do you think can pass through them?" And I heard a voice saying, "Humility."

Anthony the Great (251-356)

Don't have Jesus Christ on your lips and the world in your hearts.

Ignatius of Antioch (d. 107)

The Annunciation
Coptic Painting

Coptic

here is but one Kingdom delivered from evil. From whence comes evil? For it is quite impossible that evil should originate from goodness. We answer, then, that evil is no thing else than absence of goodness and a lapsing from what is natural into what is unnatural: for nothing evil is natural. For all things, whatsoever God made, are very good....

By nature therefore, all things are servants of the Creator and obey Him. Whenever then, any of His creatures voluntarily rebels and becomes disobedient to his Maker, he introduces evil into himself. For evil is not any essence nor a property of essence, but an accident, that is, a voluntary deviation from what is natural into what is unnatural, which is sin.

John of Damascus (675-749)

hese days no one thinks of the fears that the future holds; no one takes to heart the day of judgment, and the wrath of God; the punishments to come upon unbelievers, and the eternal torments decreed for the faithless. Whatever a conscience would fear if it believed, our conscience, because it no longer believes, doesn't fear at all. If only it believed, it would take heed; and if it took heed, it would escape.

Cyprian of Carthage (d. 258)

If you want to "pray without ceasing" [1 Thess. 5:17], never cease to long for God. The continuation of your longing is the continuation of your prayer; and if you cease to long for Him, this prayer will also cease.

Augustine of Hippo (354-430)

Our meditation in this present life should be in the praise of God; for the external exultation of our life hereafter will be the praise of God; and none can become fit for the future life who has not practiced himself for it now.

Augustine of Hippo (354-430)

Learn to pray to God in such a way that you are trusting Him as your Physician to do what He knows is best. Confess to Him the disease, and let Him choose the remedy. Then hold tight to love, for what He does will cut and sting you.

Augustine of Hippo (354-430)

The contemplation of God is promised to us as the goal of all our acts and the eternal consummation of all our joys.

Augustine of Hippo (354-430)

We don't walk to God with the feet of our body, nor would wings, if we had them, carry us to Him; but we go to Him by the affections of our soul.

Augustine of Hippo (354-430)

Page from the Book of Kells
Celtic

*I*t is due to the greed of the soul that it wants to grasp and possess many things, and thus it lays hold of time and corporeality and multiplicity, and loses precisely what it possesses.... These things must come out if God is to enter.

Augustine of Hippo (354-430)

*T*he fear of God prepares a place for love. But once love has begun to dwell in our hearts, the fear that prepared the place for it is driven out.... In sewing, the needle introduces the thread into the cloth. The needle goes in, but the thread cannot follow unless the needle comes out first. In the same way, the fear of God first occupies our minds, but it does not remain there, because it enters only in order to introduce love.

Augustine of Hippo (354-430)

Monastery of St. Paul of Thebes, Egypt

St. Anthony's cave. Egypt

When you go to bed with a contented mind, recall the blessings and generous providence of God; be filled with holy thoughts and great joy. Then, while your body sleeps, your soul will keep watch; the closing of your eyes will bring you a true vision of God; your silence will be pregnant with sanctity, and in your sleep you will continue to glorify the God of all with the full strength of your soul.

Anthony the Great (251-356)

No one should feel secure in this life, because the whole of it is one long test; and no one who is able to pass from a worse state to a better one can be certain that he will not later also pass from a better state to a worse. Our only hope, our only confidence, our only assured promise, Lord, is Your mercy.

Augustine of Hippo (354-430)

Page from the Lindisfarne Gospels
Celtic

He is truly happy who has all that he wishes to have, and wishes to have nothing that he ought not to wish.

Augustine of Hippo (354-430)

For anyone who reflects, the appearances of beauty become the themes of an invisible harmony. Perfumes as they strike our senses represent spiritual illumination. Material lights point to that immaterial Light of which they are the images.

Dionysius the Areopagite (d. 95)

od is not dependent on anything for His beauty; His beauty is not limited to certain times or aspects; but He is beautiful by Himself, through Himself, and in Himself. He is eternal beauty— not changing from one moment to the next—constantly the same beyond all change or alteration, increase or addition.

Gregory of Nyssa (330-395)

y divine grace, the universe was called by the Greeks "cosmos," meaning ornament.... Surely the author of all created beauty must Himself be the Beauty of all beauty?

Hilary of Poitiers (315-367)

od's Providence controls the universe. It is present everywhere. Providence is the sovereign Logos of God, imprinting form on the unformed materiality of the world, making and fashioning all things. Matter could not have acquired an articulated structure were it not for the directing power of the Logos who is the Image, Intellect, Wisdom and Providence of God.

Anthony the Great (251-356)

here is a mirror, a spiritual one… that not only shows us our own deformity, but transforms it too—if we are willing—into surpassing beauty. This mirror is the memory of good men, and the history of their blessed lives, the reading of the Scriptures, [and] the laws given by God.

John Chrysostom (347-407)

God not only produced the creation, but He holds together what He produced. Whether you are speaking about angels, archangels, the powers above, or simply about every creature both visible and invisible, they all enjoy the benefit of His providence. And if they are ever deprived of that providential action, they waste away, they perish, they are gone.

John Chrysostom (347-407)

Imagine your anger to be a kind of wild beast...because it too has ferocious teeth and claws, and if you don't tame it, it will devastate all things....It not only hurts the body; it even corrupts the health of the soul, devouring, rending, tearing to pieces all its strength, and making it useless for everything.

John Chrysostom (347 - 407)

When we are tempted to utter a sinful word, or when we find ourselves being carried away by anger or some other such passion, let us reflect on what privileges we have been granted, what Spirit it is whose presence we enjoy, and this thought will check in us those unruly passions.

John Chrysostom (347-407)

To the good man, to die is gain. The foolish fear death as the greatest of evils; the wise desire it as a rest after labors and the end of ills.

Ambrose of Milan (340-397)

The Flight into Egypt
Coptic Painting

Everyone who has truly been clothed in humility becomes like Him who came down from His exalted place and hid the splendor of His majesty, concealing His glory in lowliness, so that the created world should not be utterly consumed at the sight of Him....

Creation could not behold him unless he took part of it to himself and thus conversed with it; only thus was creation able to hear the words of his mouth face to face....

No one ever hates, or wounds with words, or despises the person who is humble; and because his Lord loves him, he is dear to all. Everyone loves him, everyone cherishes him, and wherever he approaches, people look on him as an angel of light and accord honor to him....

Isaac the Syrian (7th century)

It is needful also to make use of Tradition, for not everything can be gotten from sacred Scripture. The holy Apostles handed down some things in the Scriptures, other things in Tradition.

Epiphanius of Salamis (310-403)

*Archangel Gabriel
Abyssinian*

he icon is a hymn of triumph, a showing forth, a memorial inscribed for those who have fought and conquered, humbling the demons and putting them to flight.

John of Damascus (675-749)

When someone whose mind is but partially developed sees something clothed in some semblance of beauty, he believes that this thing is beautiful in its own nature. But someone who has purified the eyes of his soul and is trained to see beautiful things ... makes use of the visible as a springboard to rise to the contemplation of the spiritual.

Gregory of Nyssa (330-395)

Even if we make images of pious men, it is not so that we might adore them as gods, but that when we see them, we might be prompted to imitate them; and if we make images of Christ, it is so that our minds might soar aloft in yearning for Him.

Cyril of Alexandria (412-444)

God is the unchanging conductor as well as the unchanged Creator of all things that change. When He adds, abolishes, controls, increases or diminishes the rites of any age, He is ordering all events according to His Providence, until the beauty of the completed course of time, whose parts are the dispensations suitable to each different period, shall have played itself out, like the great melody of some ineffable composer.

Augustine of Hippo (354-430)

God is self-existent, enclosing all things and enclosed by none; within all things according to His goodness and power, and yet without all [things] in His proper nature.

Athanasius (297-373)

Understand that you have within yourself, upon a small scale, a second universe: within you is a sun, there is a moon, and there are also stars.

Origen (185-254)

With God nothing is empty of meaning, and nothing is without symbolism.

Irenaeus of Lyons (129-203)

God always was, and always is, and always will be; or rather, God always is, for "was" and "will be" are portions of time as we reckon it, and are of a changing nature. He, however, is Eternal Being.... He gathers in Himself the whole of being, because He neither has beginning nor will He have an end. He is like some great Sea of Being, limitless and unbounded, transcending every conception of time and nature.

Gregory Nazianzus (329-389)

Know that this soul of yours is free, self-determining, the fairest work of God, made according to the image of its Creator, immortal because of God who makes it immortal, a living being, rational, imperishable, because of Him who has conferred these gifts; having power to do as it will.

Cyril of Jerusalem (315-386)

The Last Judgment
The Gospel Book of
Triere

Monastery of the Archangel Gabriel
Fayoum, Egypt

If a man cannot bear being reviled, he will not see glory. If he is not cleansed of bitterness, he will not savor sweetness.

Barsanuphius (d. 550)

The Divine Nature has the property of penetrating all things without mixing with them and of being Itself impenetrable by anything else.

John of Damascus (675-749)

Conscience and reputation are two things. Conscience is due to yourself; reputation is due to your neighbor.

Augustine of Hippo (354-430)

In doing what we ought, we deserve no praise, because it is our duty.

Augustine of Hippo (354-430)

St. Catherine's Monastery
Mount Sinai, Egypt

I cannot show you my God, but I can show you His works. "Everything was made by Him" (John 1:3). He created the world in its newness, He who has no beginning. He who is eternal created time. He who is unmoved made movement. Look at His works and praise their Maker.

Augustine of Hippo (354-430)

One way of coming to knowledge of God is that which is provided by the whole of creation; and another, no less significant, is that which is offered by conscience, the whole of which we have expounded upon at great length, showing how you have a self-taught knowledge of what is good and what is not so good, and how conscience urges all this upon you from within. Two teachers, then, are given you from the beginning: creation and conscience. Neither of them has voice to speak out; yet they teach men in silence.

John Chrysostom (347-407)

For when he considers the universe, can anyone be so simple minded as not to believe that the Divine is present in everything, pervading, embracing, and penetrating it? For all things depend upon Him Who is, and nothing can exist which does not have its being in Him Who is.

Gregory of Nyssa (330-395)

God is within all, over all, under all, is both above with His power and beneath with His support, exterior in respect to magnitude and interior in respect to subtlety, extending from the heights to the depths, encompassing the outside and penetrating the inside; but He is not in one part above, in another beneath, nor in one part exterior and in another interior. Rather, one and the same wholly and everywhere, He supports in presiding and presides in supporting, penetrates in encompassing and encompasses in penetrating.

Gregory the Great (Pope) (540-604)

Whoever does not trust the Lord in small matters is quite clearly an unbeliever in things of greater importance.

Basil the Great (329-379)

Every visible or invisible creature is a theophany or appearance of God. The Christian is the one who, wherever he looks, sees God everywhere and rejoices in Him.... Man is the microcosm in the strictest sense of the word. He is the summary of all existence. There is no creature that is not recapitulated in man. There is nothing in the universe that is lower than body or higher than soul.

John Scotus Eriugena (810-877)

Christ, the Virgin, and St. Mark
San Marco, Venice

Like a musician who has tuned his lyre, and by the artistic blending of low and high and medium tones produces a single melody, so the Wisdom of God, holding the universe like a lyre, adapting things heavenly to things earthly, and earthly things to heavenly, harmonizes them all, and leading them by His will, makes one world and one world order in beauty and harmony.

Athanasius (296-373)

The Crucifixion
Romanesque

Ⓖod is over all things, under all things, outside all; within but not enclosed; without but not excluded; above but not raised up; below but not depressed; wholly above, presiding; wholly beneath, sustaining; wholly without, embracing; wholly within, filling.

Hildebert of Lavardin (ca. 1056 - ca. 1133)

Study your heart in the light of the Holy Scriptures, and you will know therein who you were, who you are, and who you ought to be.

Fulgence of Ruspe (468 - 533)

Throughout the entire creation, the manifest wisdom of God shines forth from Him and in Him, as in a mirror containing the beauty of all forms and lights and as in a book in which all things are written according to the deep secrets of God. O, if only I could find this book whose origin is eternal, whose essence is incorruptible, whose knowledge is life, whose script is indelible, whose study is desirable, whose teaching is easy, whose knowledge is sweet, whose depth is inscrutable, whose words are ineffable, yet all are a single Word! Truly, whoever finds this book will find life and will draw salvation from the Lord.

Bonaventure (1217 - 1274)

Pepin's Reliquary
Aveyron, France

know that the Immovable comes down;
I know that the Invisible appears to me;
I know that He who is far outside the whole creation
   Takes me within Himself and hides me in His arms,
   And then I find myself outside the world.
I, a frail, small mortal in the world,
Behold the Creator of the world, all of Him, within myself;
   And I know that I shall not die,
   For I am within the Life,
I have the whole of life springing up as a fountain within me.
He is in my heart, He is in heaven:
Both there and here He shows Himself to me with equal glory.

John Scotus Eriugena (810-877)

he high and the low of all creation, God gives to humankind to use. If this privilege is misused, God's justice permits creation to punish humanity.

Hildegard of Bingen (1098-1179)

f you were to look at every creature from the beginning of creation to the end of time, whether it were the most radiant angel or the tiniest worm, you would see in it signs of God's goodness and His overflowing love.

Aelred of Rievaulx (1110-1167)

I pray God may open your eyes and let you see what hidden treasures He bestows on us in the trials from which the world thinks only to flee.

John of Avila (1499-1569)

Anyone who wants to practice perfect poverty must renounce all worldly wisdom and even secular learning, to a certain extent. Divested of these possessions, he will be able to make the great acts of God his theme and offer himself naked to the embrace of the Crucified. Anyone who clings to his own opinions in the depths of his heart has not renounced the world perfectly.

Francis of Assisi (1182-1226)

These creatures minister to our needs every day: without them we could not live; and through them the human race greatly offends the Creator. Every day we fail to appreciate so great a blessing by not praising as we should the Creator and Dispenser of all these gifts.

Francis of Assisi (1182-1226)

When you have stabilized your heart in right faith, and steadfast hope, and perfect love, then you will heave up your heart in high contemplation of your Creator.

Edmund of Abingdon (1175-1240)

Christ saves Peter from the sea
Byzantine mosaic

ust as at sea, those who are carried away from the direction of the harbor bring themselves back on course by a clear sign, so Scripture may guide those adrift on the sea of life back into the harbor of the Divine Will.

Gregory of Nyssa (330-395)

The [physical and spiritual] worlds are one. For the spiritual world in its totality is manifested in the totality of the perceptible world, mystically expressed in symbolic pictures for those who have eyes to see. And the perceptible world in its entirety is secretly fathomable by the spiritual world in its entirety.... The former is embodied in the latter through the realities; the latter in the former through the symbols. The operation of the two is one.

Maximus the Confessor (580-662)

So long as [a human being's] will is stubborn and raw, [God] abandons him to the domination of evil; for he has chosen the shameful passions of which the devil is the sower, in preference to nature, of which God is the creator. God leaves him free to incline, if he so wishes, towards the passions of the flesh, and actually to satisfy that inclination. Valuing the insubstantial passions more highly than nature, in his concern for these passions he has become ignorant of the principle of nature. Had he followed that principle, he would have known what constitutes the law of nature and what constitutes the tyranny of the passions—a tyranny brought about, not by nature, but by deliberate choice. He would then have accepted the law of nature that is maintained through activities which are natural; and he would have expelled the tyranny of the passions completely from his will. He would have obeyed nature with his intelligence, for nature in itself is pure and undefiled, faultless, free from hatred and alienation, and he would have made his will once more a companion of nature, totally stripped of everything not bestowed by the principle of nature. In this way he would have eradicated all hatred for and all alienation from what is by nature akin to him.

Maximus the Confessor (580-662)

The Chora Church, Istanbul
Byzantine

Jf, instead of stopping short at the outward appearance which visible things present to the senses, you seek with your intellect to contemplate their inner essences, seeing them as images of spiritual realities or as the inward principles of sensible objects, you will be taught that nothing belonging to the visible world is unclean. For by nature all things were created good.

Maximus the Confessor (580-662)

A true teacher is he who through his all-embracing cognitive thought comprehends created things concisely, as if they constituted a single body, establishing distinctions and connections between them according to their generic difference and identity, so as to indicate which possess similar qualities.... Or again, a true spiritual teacher is he who distinguishes and relates the general and universal qualities of created things—classified in accordance with a formulation that embraces everything....

A true philosopher is one who perceives in created things their spiritual Cause, or who knows created things through knowing their Cause, having attained a union with God that transcends the intellect and a direct, unmediated faith. He does not simply learn about divine things, but actually experiences them.

A student of spiritual knowledge, though not properly speaking a philosopher, is he who esteems and studies God's wisdom mirrored in His creation, down to the least vestige of it; but he does this without any self-display or any hankering after human praise and glory, for he wishes to be a lover of God's wisdom in creation and not a lover of materialism.

Gregory of Sinai (1265-1346)

The better one is, the worse one becomes, if one attributes the cause of this goodness to one's self.

Bernard of Clairvaux (1090-1153)

When the mind, by the grace of Christ, ascends to what is above nature, then it is enlightened by the illumination of the Holy Spirit and splendidly reaches out into contemplation. And having come above itself, according to the measurement of grace given to it by God, it clearly and purely beholds the nature of all things in accordance with its condition and order.

Gregory Palamas
(1296-1359)

St. Vitale's vault
Ravenna
Byzantine

he whole of this present world has become mean and wearisome, and on the other hand the world to come has become so unspeakably desirable and dear that I hold all these passing things as light as thistledown.

Herman of Reichenau (1013-1054)

The day of my spiritual awakening was the day I saw, and knew I saw, all things in God and God in all things.

Mechthild of Magdeburg (1210-1285)

If things created are so full of loveliness, how resplendent with beauty must be the One who made them! The wisdom of the Worker is apparent in His handiwork.

Anthony of Padua (1195-1231)

No single creature can express in full manner the likeness of God: it cannot be equal to God. The presence of multiplicity and variety among created things was therefore necessary that a perfect likeness to God be found in them according to their manner of being.

Albert the Great (1193-1280)

IHS · FILIAM · IAYRI · PRINCIPIS · SYNAGO
GE · IDOMO · RES VSCITAT :

Christ heals Jarius' daughter
Palermo
Byzantine mosaic

hoever is anxious to ascend to God must first eliminate nature-deforming sins, and then train the mind by prayer, to receive reforming grace; by a good life, to receive purifying righteousness; by contemplation, to receive perfecting wisdom. And no one can receive wisdom except through grace, righteousness and knowledge. Likewise, no one can achieve contemplation except through penetrating meditation, a holy life and devout prayer.

By the first method, man considers things in themselves, and sees in them weight, number and measure, and so determines their composition. Thus, man sees in them mode, species and order, as well as substance, power and operation. From these, as from so many traces, he can rise to the understanding of the immeasurable power, wisdom and goodness of the Creator.

By the second method, man considers the world in its origin, development and end. By faith we understand that the world was fashioned by the Word of God. By faith we believe that three phases of law succeeded each other and ran their course in perfect order: the law of nature, the law of Scripture, and the law of grace. Thus are displayed, first the power, then the providence, lastly the justice of the Supreme Principle.

By the third method, that of investigation by reason, man sees that some things possess existence only, others possess existence and life, others again, existence, life and reason. The first things he sees to be lower, the second to be intermediate, and the third to be higher. He also sees that some things are only material; others partly material and partly spiritual; from which he concludes that others still are purely spiritual....

From these things, which are subject to perception, man rises to the consideration of divine power, wisdom and goodness as something existent, alive, intelligent, purely spiritual, incorruptible and immutable.

This reasoning may be developed in accordance with the sevenfold characteristics of creatures, which are a sevenfold testimony to the power, wisdom and goodness of God: that is, by considering the origin, vastness, multitude, beauty, fullness, operation, and order of things.

Bonaventure (1217-1274)

Creation out of nothing implies, on the part of the creature, a state of being subsequent upon a state of non-being, and, on the part of the Principle, a boundless productive power, which is found in God alone. Necessarily then the universe must be created in time by this same boundless power in acting in Itself and without intermediary.

Bonaventure (1217-1274)

In everything, whether it is a thing sensed or a thing known, God Himself is hidden within.

Bonaventure (1217-1274)

The Crucifixion
St. Catherine's Monastery
Mount Sinai, Egypt

St. Apollinare in Classe
Ravenna
Byzantine mosaic

All things flow constantly from God, as water flows from a spring, and tends ever to return to Him as water tends ever to return to its level.

John Scotus Eriugena (810-877)

 o not denigrate anything God has created. All creation is simple, plain and good. And God is present throughout His creation. Why do you ever consider things beneath your notice? God's justice is to be found in every detail of what He has made. The human race alone is capable of injustice. Human beings alone are capable of disobeying God's laws, because they try to be wiser than God....

The rest of creation cries out against the evil and perversity of the human species. Other creatures fulfill the commandments of God; they honor His laws. And other creatures do not grumble and complain about those laws. But human beings rebel against those laws, defying them in word and action. And in doing so they inflict terrible cruelty on the rest of God's creation.

Hildegard of Bingen (1098-1179)

true lover of wisdom is he who, through natural things, has learned to know their Creator, and from the Creator, has understood natural things and things Divine; and such as knows not from teaching only, but from experience. Or, a perfect lover of wisdom is he who has perfected himself in the moral, natural and Divine love of wisdom, or rather, in love of God.

Gregory of Sinai (1265-1346)

Try to realize the dignity which God has conferred on you. He created and formed your body in the image of His beloved Son, and you are made in His own likeness. And yet every creature under heaven serves and acknowledges and obeys its Creator in its own way better than you do.

Francis of Assisi (1182-1226)

We can never know how patient or humble someone is when everything is going well with him. But when those who should cooperate with him do exactly the opposite, then we can know. A man has as much patience and humility as he has then, and no more.

Francis of Assisi (1182-1226)

When a man envies his brother the good that God says or does through him, it is like committing a sin of blasphemy, because he is really envying God, who is the only source of every good.

Francis of Assisi (1182-1226)

Romanesque
Madonna

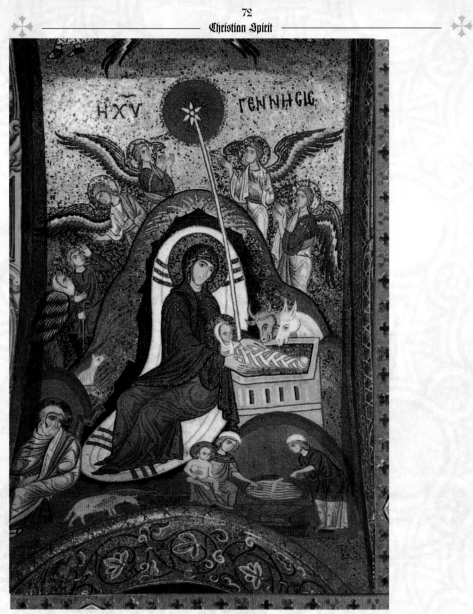

The Nativity, Church of Martorana, Palermo
Byzantine mosaic

Keep in mind that each of you has your own vineyard. But every one is joined to your neighbors' vineyards without any dividing lines. They are also joined together, in fact, that you cannot do good or evil for yourself without also doing the same for your neighbors.

All of you together make up one common vineyard, the whole Christian assembly, and you are all united in the vineyard of the mystic body of holy Church from which you draw your life. In this vineyard is planted the vine, which is My only-begotten Son, into Whom you must be engrafted. Unless you are engrafted into Him, you are rebels against the holy Church.

Catherine of Siena (1347-1380)

The earth is full of Thy creation." Of what creation of Thine is the earth full? Of all trees and shrubs, of all animals and flocks, and of the whole of the human race; the earth is full of the creation of God. We see, now, read, recognize, praise and in these we preach of Him; yet we are not able to praise respecting these things, as fully as our heart doth abound with praise after the beautiful contemplation of them.

Augustine of Hippo (354-430)

The crown of victory is promised only to those who engage in the struggle.

Augustine of Hippo (354-430)

*T*he saints have no need of honor from us; neither does our devotion add the slightest thing to what is theirs. Clearly, if we venerate their memory, it serves us, not them. But I tell you, when I think of them, I feel myself inflamed by tremendous yearning.

Bernard of Clairvaux (1090-1153)

*D*iscernment is the light which dissolves all darkness, dissipates ignorance, and seasons every virtue and virtuous deed. It has a prudence that cannot be deceived, a strength that is invincible, a constancy right up to the end, reaching as it does from heaven to earth; that is, from the knowledge of Me to the knowledge of oneself, from love of Me to love of one's neighbors.

It would never be right to offend Me, infinite Good, under the pretext of saving My finite creation. The evil would far outweigh any fruit that might come of it, so never, for any reason, must you sin. True charity knows this, for it always carries the lamp of holy discernment.

Catherine of Siena (1347-1380)

*G*od said: I have placed you in the midst of your fellows that you may do to them what you cannot do to Me—that is, so that you may love your neighbor freely without expecting any return from him. And what you do to him I count as done to Me.

Catherine of Siena (1347-1380)

Christ, the Virgin, and St. John the Baptist
Hagia Sophia, Istanbul
Byzantine

It is God's way to care for all His creatures, both the greatest and the least. We should likewise care for creatures, whatsoever they are, in the sense that we use them in conformity with the divine purpose, in order that they may not bear witness against us in the Day of Judgment.

Thomas Aquinas (1225-1274)

mong all human pursuits, the pursuit of wisdom is more perfect, more noble, more useful, and more full of joy.

Thomas Aquinas (1225-1274)

creature is a letter written by the finger of God, and many creatures, like many letters, make up a book. The book of nature, however, is superior to the book of scripture: it cannot be falsified, destroyed, or misinterpreted; it will not induce heresy, and heretics cannot misunderstand it.

Ramon Sibiude (1378-1438)

od creates everything, but He remains uncreated. The fact that the world has a beginning is confirmed by nature and taught us by history.... Creation is not from God's essence; it is not the uncreated energies of God, but the result of the uncreated energies.... To "beget" is the property of God's nature, but to "create" is the property of His energy and will. If there were no distinction between essence and energies, between nature and will, then the creatures would belong by nature to God....

Man is animal in his body, but his soul originated in the transcendental world (hyperkosmion) and is a superior creation. Man was made paradoxically a small world (mikrokosmos) in which is summarized all the rest of creation. For this reason He created man to stand between, to include and to beautify, both worlds, the visible and the invisible.

Gregory Palamas (1296-1359)

he following words, Hildegard says, were dictated to her by the Holy Spirit: I, the highest and fiery power, have kindled every living spark, and I have breathed out nothing that can die.... I am the fiery life of the Divine Essence—the flame above the beauty of the fields; I shine in the waters; in the sun, the moon and the stars. I burn. And by means of the airy wind, I stir everything into quickness with certain invisible life which sustains all. For the air lives in its "green" power and its blossoming; the waters flow as if they were alive. Even the sun is alive in its own light. I, the fiery power, lie hidden in these things and they blaze from Me, just as man is continually moved by his breath, and as the fire contains the nimble flame. All these things live in their own essence and are without death, since I am life... I am the whole of life—life was not torn from stones; it did not bud from branches; nor is it rooted in the generative power of the male. Rather, every living thing is rooted in Me.

Hildegard of Bingen (1098-1179)

he pleasant companionship of all the blessed in heaven will be a companionship replete with delight. For each one will possess all good things together with the blessed, because they will love one another as themselves, and therefore will rejoice in the happiness of others' goods as well as their own. Consequently, the joy and gladness of one will be as great as the joy of all.

Thomas Aquinas (1225-1274)

The Crucifixion
Basilica of St. Clemente, Rome

Monastery at Daphne, Greece
Byzantine

We are not to suppose that the existence of things is caused by God in the same way as the existence of a house is caused by its builder. When the builder departs, the house still remains standing.... But God is, directly, by Himself, the cause of the very existence, and communicates existence to all things just as the sun communicates light to the air and to whatever else is illuminated by the sun. The continuous shining of the sun is required for the preservation of light in the air; similarly God must confer existence on all things if they are to persevere in existence.... Therefore, God must be in all things.

Thomas Aquinas (1225-1274)

Fresco at San Marco, Venice
Byzantine

If someone, at the Devil's prompting, had committed every sin against God and then, with true contrition and the intention of amendment, truly repented these sins and humbly, with burning love, asked God for mercy, there is no doubt that the kind and merciful God Himself would immediately be as ready to receive that person back into His grace with great joy and happiness as would be a loving father who saw returning to him his only, dearly beloved son, now freed from a great scandal and a most shameful death.

Bridget of Sweden (1303-1373)

God showed me in my palm a little thing round as a ball about the size of a hazelnut. I looked at it with the eye of my understanding and asked myself: "What is this thing ?" And I was answered: "It is everything that is created." I wondered how it could survive since it seemed so little that it could suddenly disintegrate into nothing. The answer came: "It endures and ever will endure, because God loves it." And so everything has being because of God's love.

Julian of Norwich (1342-1423)

Fresco at San Marco, Venice
Byzantine

The Khan Madonna
Byzantine

ur self-will is so subtle and so deeply rooted within us, so covered with excuses and defended by false reasoning, that it seems to be a demon. When we cannot do our own will in one way, we do it in another, under all kinds of pretexts.

Catherine of Genoa (1447-1510)

et everyone who has the grace of intelligence fear that, because of it, he will be judged more heavily if he is negligent. Let him who has no intelligence or talent rejoice and do as much as he can with the little that he has; for he has been freed from many occasions of sin.

Bridget of Sweden (1303-1373)

o have the material things of the world is not sinful. After all, everything is good and perfect, made by Me, Goodness Itself. But I made these things to serve My rational creatures; I did not intend My creatures to make themselves servants and slaves to the world's pleasures. They owe their first love to Me. Everything else they should love and possess, as I told you, not as if they owned it, but as something lent them.

Catherine of Siena (1347-1380)

To know whom to avoid is a great means of saving our souls.

Thomas Aquinas (1225-1274)

As the soul becomes more pure and bare and poor, and possesses less of created things, and is emptied of all things that are not God, it receives God more purely, and is more completely in Him; and it truly becomes one with God, and it looks into God, and God into it, face to face as it were; two images transformed into one. Some simple folk think that they will see God as if He were standing there and they here. It is not so. God and I, we are one.

Meister Eckhart (1260-1327)

There are two sides to every sin: the turning of the will toward fleeting satisfaction and the turning away from everlasting value. As regards the first, the principle of all sins can be called lust — lust in its most general sense, namely, the unbridled desire for one's own pleasure. As regards the second, the principle is pride — pride in its general sense, the lack of submission to God.

Thomas Aquinas (1225-1274)

Christ Pantocrator
St. Julien's Basilica
Brioude, France

f there is anyone who is not enlightened by this sublime magnificence of created things, he is blind.... If there is anyone who, seeking all these works of God, does not praise Him, he is dumb; if there is anyone who, from so many signs, cannot perceive God, that man is foolish.

Bonaventure (1221-1274)

Romanesque cloister
Le Puy, France

nly he to whom God is present in everything and who employs his reason in the highest degree and has enjoyment in it knows anything of true peace and has a real kingdom of heaven.

Meister Eckhart (1260-1327)

o not be concerned about the style of your food and clothing, thus laying too much stress on them, but rather accustom your heart and mind to be exalted above such things, so that nothing may move you to pleasure or to love except God alone.

Meister Eckhart (1260-1327)

od is closer to me than I am to myself: my being depends on God's being near me and present to me. So He is also in a stone or a log of wood, only they do not know.... So man is more blessed than a stone or a piece of wood because he is aware of God and knows how close God is to him. And I am more blessed, the more I realize this.

Meister Eckhart (1260-1327)

acred writings are bound into two volumes: that of creation and that of Holy Scripture.

Thomas Aquinas (1225-1274)

aith is a luminous star that leads the honest seeker into the mysteries of nature. You must seek your point of affinity in God, and put your trust into an honest, divine, sincere, pure and strong faith, and cling to it with your whole heart, soul, sense and thought—full of love and confidence. If you possess such a faith, God's wisdom will not withhold Truth from you, but He will reveal His works to you credibly, visibly and consolingly.

Paracelsus (1493-1541)

od in the macrocosm and God in the microcosm are one, for there is only one God, and one law and one nature, through which Wisdom becomes manifest.... The more the soul of man grows perfect, the nearer does it approach to God, and the more will his understanding grow and his love be exalted. Thus may man elevate himself into sanctification; he may communicate with perfect beings in the spiritual kingdom and be instructed and guided by them. He will be a true child of God. All nature will be subject to him because he will be an instrument to carry out the will of the Creator of nature.

Paracelsus (1493-1541)

Everyone – past, present and future – will be judged.... Now, then, is the time for mercy, while the time to come will be the time for justice only. For that reason, the present time is ours, but the future time will be God's only.

Thomas Aquinas
(1225-1274)

The Virgin
San Marco, Venice
Byzantine

he entire universe pre-exists in the Godhead, which is its primordial cause. Father, Son, and Holy Spirit are all in all, because in Their divinity every other thing is anticipated and possessed.

Thomas Aquinas (1225-1274)

ll that the earth issues forth ... is connected and bound to God.... The earth is at the same time mother. She is mother of all, for contained in her are the seeds of all. The earth of humankind contains all moistness, all verdancy, all germinating power. It is in so many ways fruitful. All the other parts of creation come from it. Yet it forms not only the basic raw material for humankind, but also the substance of the incarnation of God's Son.

Hildegard of Bingen (1098-1179)

f we should see two men fighting together over serious matters, we would still think them both crazy if they did not leave off fighting when they saw a ferocious lion coming toward them, ready to devour them both. Now considering that we surely see that death is coming on us all, and will undoubtedly within a short time devour us all—how soon, we don't know—isn't it worse than insanity to be angry and bear malice to one another, more often than not over trivial matters, in the same way children fight over cherry stones?

Thomas More (1477-1535)

Gothic cloister
Haute Rive, Switzerland

It is not necessary for us to set forth our petitions before God in order to make known to Him our needs and desires, but rather that we ourselves may realize that in these things it is necessary to have recourse to God's assistance.

Thomas Aquinas (1225-1274)

nd God saw that it was good. God does not judge the beauty of His work by the charm of the eyes, and He does not hold to the same idea of beauty that we do. What He esteems beautiful is that which presents in its perfection all the fitness of art, and that which tends to the usefulness of its end....

May God who after having made such great things ... grant you the intelligence of His truth so that you may raise yourselves from visible things to the invisible Being, and that the grandeur and beauty of creatures may give you a just idea of the Creator. For the visible things of him from the creation of the world are clearly seen, and His power and divinity are eternal. Thus earth, air, sky, water, day, night, all visible things, remind us of Him who is our Benefactor.

Basil the Great (329-379)

or creation, as if written in characters and by means of its order and harmony, declares in a loud voice its own Master and Creator.... For this reason, God, by his own Word, gave creation such order as is found therein, so that while He is by nature invisible, men might yet be able to know Him through His works.

Anthony the Great (251-356)

Christ Pantocrator
Russian Orthodox

he creation proclaims outright the Creator. For the very heavens, as the Psalmist says, declare the glory of God (Psalm 19:1) with their unutterable words. We see the universal harmony in the wondrous sky and on the wondrous earth; how elements essentially opposed to each other are all woven together in an ineffable union to serve one common end, each contributing its particular force to maintain the whole....

We see all this with the piercing eyes of mind, nor can we fail to be taught by means of such a spectacle that a Divine Power, working with skill and method, is manifesting Itself in this actual world, and, penetrating each portion, combines those portions with the whole and completes the whole by the portions, and encompasses the universe with a single all-controlling force, self-centered, never ceasing from its motion, yet never altering the position which It holds.

Gregory of Nyssa (330-395)

ust as you see that a ray of light entering through a window is colored in different ways according to the different colors ... so the Divine Ray shines forth in each and every creature in different ways and in different properties....

Bonaventure (1217–1274)

The Last Supper
Greek Orthodox

Ο ΑΓΙ ΠΝΟΣ   Ο ΜΥΣΤΙΚΟΣ

Apostle Peter
Russian Orthodox

Well and good if all things change, Lord God, provided we are rooted in You.

John of the Cross (1542-1591)

It is possible to understand by every tree the knowledge of the divine power derived from created things. In the words of the divine apostle, "Since the creation of the world, His invisible nature has been clearly seen, being perceptible in the things that are made."

John of Damascus (675-749)

As it is said, "In everything gives thanks" (1 Thess. 5:18).... No matter what you do, you should keep in mind the Creator of all things.... When you see the sky, the earth, the sea and all that is in them, marvel at these things and glorify their Creator. When you put on clothing, acknowledge whose gift it is and praise Him who in His providence has given you life. In short, if everything you do becomes for you an occasion for glorifying God, you will be praying unceasingly. And in this way your soul will always rejoice.

Peter of Damascus (1027–1107)

od turns Himself away, not so much from those who sin, as from those who aren't stricken with fear after they sin.

John Chrysostom (347-407)

oor human reason, when it trusts in itself, substitutes the strangest absurdities for the highest divine concepts.

John Chrysostom (347-407)

ating and drinking don't make friendships—such friendship even robbers and murderers have. But if we are friends, if we truly care for one another, let us help one another spiritually.... Let us hinder those things that lead our friends away to hell.

John Chrysostom (347-407)

John Chrysostom
Russian Orthodox

Trinity Monastery
Vologda, Russia

ll creatures are balanced upon the Creative Word of God, as if upon a bridge of diamond. Above them is the abyss of Divine Infinitude, while below them that of their own nothingness.

Philaret of Moscow (1652-1681)

In this night of reconciliation, let none be angry or gloomy. In this night that stills everything, let nothing threaten or disturb. This night belongs to the sweet One; let nothing bitter or harsh be in it. In this night that belongs to the meek One, let there be nothing high or haughty. In this day of pardoning, let us not exact punishments for trespasses. In this day of gladness, let us not spread sadness.... In this day when God came to sinners, let not the righteous man be in his own mind uplifted over the sinner.

Ephraem the Syrian (306-373)

𝔚 isdom shining in all things invites us, with a certain foretaste of its effects, to be borne to its effects, to be borne to it with a wonderful desire. For life itself is an intellectual Spirit, having in itself a certain innate foretaste through which it searches with great desire for the very Font of its own life.

Nicholas of Cusa (1401-1464)

Do now—do now—what you'll wish you had done when your moment comes to die.

Angela Merici (1474-1540)

Lord, it behooveth me to scale that wall of invisible vision beyond which Thou art to be found. Now the wall is at one and the same time all things and nothing. For Thou, who seemest to me to be as it were all things and naught of all things at once, dwellest within that lofty wall which no genius can scale by its own power.

Nicholas of Cusa (1401-1464)

Nothing restrains anger, curbs pride, heals the wound of malice, bridles self-indulgence, quenches the passions, checks avarice and puts unclean thoughts to flight as does the name of Jesus.

Bernard of Clairvaux (1090-1153)

Be at peace with your soul; then heaven and earth will be at peace with you. Enter eagerly into the treasure house that is within you, and so you will see the things that are in heaven; for there is but one single entry to them both. The ladder that leads to the kingdom is hidden within your soul. Flee from sin, dive into yourself, and in your soul you will discover the stairs by which to ascend.

Isaac the Syrian (7th century)

The power to recognize and to follow the truth cannot be conferred by academic degrees; it comes only from God. He who desires to know the Truth must be able to see It, and not be satisfied with descriptions of It received from others.

Paracelsus (1493-1541)

We may gain some inkling of what God is if we attempt by means of every sensation to reach the reality of each creature, not giving up until we are alive to what transcends it....

Clement of Alexandria (d. 215)

The Vladimir Virgin
Russian Orthodox

The Holy Trinity Cathedral, Kostroma
Russian Orthodox

e not anxious over anything; but in every thing by prayer and supplication with thanksgiving let your requests be made known unto God. And the peace of God, which passeth all understanding, shall keep your hearts and minds through Christ Jesus.

Philippians 4:6-7

he one who gazes on the physical universe and perceives the wisdom which is reflected in the beauty of created realities, can reason from the visible to the invisible beauty, the Source of Wisdom, whose influence established the nature of all reality. So also can one who looks upon this new universe of creation which is the Church see in it the One who is all in all, and thus be led by our faith from things which are intelligible and understandable to a knowledge of the One who is beyond all knowledge.

Gregory of Nyssa (330-395)

reation is a system and compound of earth and sky and all that is in them, an admirable creation indeed when we look at the beautiful form of every part, but yet more worthy of admiration when we consider the harmony and unison of the whole, and how each part fits with every other in fair order, and all with the whole, tending to the perfect completion of the world as a unit.

Gregory Nazianzus (329-390)

teacher initiated into things divine is one who can distinguish principal beings from participative beings, or beings that have no autonomous self-subsistent reality.... Inspired by the Holy Spirit, he perceives the essences of principal beings embodied in participative beings. In other words, he interprets what is intelligible and invisible in terms of what is sensible and visible, and the visible sense-world in terms of the invisible and supra-sensory world, conscious that what is invisible is the archetype of what is visible. He knows that things possessing form and pattern are brought

into being by what is formless and without pattern, and that each manifests the other spiritually; and he clearly perceives each in the other and conveys this perception in his teaching of the truth. His knowledge of the truth, with all its sun-like radiance, is not expressed in allegorical form; on the contrary, he elucidates the true underlying principles of both worlds with spiritual insight and power, and expounds them forcefully and vividly. In this way the visible world becomes our teacher, and the invisible world is shown to be an eternal divine dwelling-place....

Gregory of Sinai (1265-1346)

Shrine Cross, Russian Orthodox

Gennadij of Kostroma
Russian Orthodox

ature is school-mistress, the soul the pupil; and whatever one has taught or the other has learned has come from God — the Teacher of the teacher.

Clement of Alexandria (150-220)

or the name Adam ... is not now given to a created object. For created man has no special name; he is universal man, encompassing in himself all of humanity. So then, by this designation of Adam's universal nature, we are led to understand that Divine Providence and Energy embrace in primordial creation the whole human race. For God's image is not confined to one part of nature, nor grace to only one individual among those belonging to it.... There is no distinction between man formed at the beginning of the world's creation, and him who will come at the end: they bear in themselves the same image of God. Consequently, man, made in God's image, is nature understood as a whole, reflecting the likeness of God. God's image, proper to Adam's person, relates to all of humanity, to "universal man."

Gregory of Nyssa (330-395)

iscipline, the safeguard of hope, the bond of faith, the guide of the way of salvation, the stimulus and nourishment of good dispositions, the teacher of virtue, causes us to abide always in Christ, and to live continually for God, and to attain to the heavenly promises and to the divine rewards. To follow her is wholesome, and to turn away from her and neglect her is deadly.

Cyprian of Carthage (d. 258)

or what purpose does He (Jesus) go up into the mountain? To teach us that loneliness and retirement is good when we are to pray to God. With this view, you see, He is continually withdrawing into the wilderness, and there often spends the whole night in prayer, teaching us earnestly to seek such quiet in our prayers, as the time and place may confer. For the wilderness is the mother of quiet; it is a calm and a harbor, delivering us from all turmoil.

John Chrysostom (347-407)

od's providence embraces the whole universe.... By contemplating the beauty and use of each thing, (one who has acquired the habit of detachment) is filled with love for the Creator. He surveys all visible things: the sky, the sun, moon, stars and clouds, rain, snow and hail ... thunder, lightning, the winds and breezes and the way they change, the seasons, the years...; the four-legged animals, the wild beasts and animals and reptiles, all the birds, the springs and rivers, the many varieties of plants and herbs, both wild and cultivated. He sees in all things the order, the equilibrium, the proportion, the beauty, the rhythm, the union, the harmony, the usefulness, the variety, the motion, the colors, the shapes, the reversion of things to their source, permanence in the midst of corruption. Contemplating thus all created realities, he is filled with wonder.

Peter of Damascus (1027–1107)

od created everything, not only for our use, but also that we, seeing the great wealth of His creations, might be astonished at the might of the Creator and might understand that all this was created with wisdom and unutterable goodness, for the honor of man, who was to appear.

John Chrysostom (347-407)

The Transfiguration Cathedral, Kizhi Island
Russian Orthodox

he greater the charity of the saints in their heavenly home, the more they intercede for those who are still on their journey and the more they can help them by their prayers; the more they are united with God, the more effective those prayers are. This is in accordance with divine order, which makes higher things react upon lower things, like the brightness of the sun filling the atmosphere.

Thomas Aquinas (1225-1274)

f your speech is full of wisdom and you meditate on understanding in your heart (cf. Psalm 49:3), you will discover in created things the presence of the divine Logos, the substantive Wisdom of God the Father (cf. 1 Corinthians 1:24); for in created things you will perceive the outward expression of the archetypes that characterize them, and thus through your active living intelligence, you will speak wisdom that derives from the Divine Wisdom.

Gregory of Sinai (1265-1346)

The Virgin Praying
Russian Orthodox

e must busy ourselves with preparations for our departure from this world. For even if the day when the whole world ends never overtakes us, the end of each of us is right at the door.

John Chrysostom (347-407)

he Divine Nature is impossible to see with eyes of flesh: but from the works, which are Divine, it is possible to attain to some conception of His power, according to Solomon, who says, "For by the greatness and beauty of the creatures proportionately the Maker of them is seen" (Wisdom 13:5). For God appears the greater to every man in proportion as he has grasped a larger survey of the creatures: and when his heart is lifted up by that larger survey, he gains withal a greater conception of God.

Cyril of Jerusalem (315-386)

ouls that love truth and God, that long with much hope and faith to put on Christ completely, do not need so much to be put in remembrance by others, nor do they endure, even for a while, to be deprived of the heavenly desire and of passionate affection to the Lord; but being wholly and entirely nailed to the cross of Christ, they perceive in themselves day by day a sense of spiritual advance towards the spiritual Bridegroom.

Macarius the Great (300-390)

St. Sophia, Novgorod
Russian Orthodox

nger, fear, cowardice, arrogance, pleasure, grief, hatred, spite, heartless cruelty, jealousy, flattery, bearing grudges and resentment, and all the other hostile drives within us: There is your array of the masters and tyrants that try to enslave the soul, their prisoner of war, and bring it under their control.

Gregory of Nyssa (330-395)

od, full beyond measure, brought creatures into being, not because He had need of anything, but so that they might participate in Him in proportion to their capacity, and that He Himself might rejoice in His works, through seeing them joyful and ever filled to overflowing with His inexhaustible gifts.

Maximus the Confessor (580-662)

Metropolitan Alekssej
Russian Orthodox

or man's sake God has created everything: earth and heaven and the beauty of the stars. Men cultivate the earth for themselves, but if they fail to recognize how great is God's Providence, their souls lack all spiritual understanding.

Anthony the Great (251-356)

hatever ye do, do all to the glory of God.

1 Corinthians 10:31

This man He (God) set upon the earth as a kind of second world, a microcosm; another kind of angel…. He was king of all upon the earth, but a subject of heaven; earthly and heavenly, transient yet immortal; belonging both to the visible and to the intelligible order…; combining in the same being spirit and flesh…. Thus he is a living creature under God's Providence here, while in transition to another state and … in process of deification by reason of his natural tendency toward God.

Gregory Nazianzus (329-389)

Contemplating the visible things of God's power and providence, His goodness and wisdom, as Paul says (Romans 1: 20-21), and perceiving the mysteries hidden in the divine Scriptures, [the one whose intellect has been purified] is given the grace to ascend with Christ through the contemplation of intelligible realities…. Perceiving the invisible through the visible, and the eternal through the transitory, he realizes that if this ephemeral world … is so beautiful, how much more beautiful must be the eternal, inconceivable blessings "that God has prepared for those who love Him" (1 Corinthians 2:9).

Peter of Damascus (1027–1107)

Our Lady of the Consolation
Greek Orthodox

Blessed is the mind that, passing by all creatures, constantly rejoices in God's beauty.

Maximus the Confessor
(580-662)

A right view of created things depends upon a truly spiritual knowledge of visible and invisible realities. Visible realities are objects perceived by the senses, while invisible realities are poetic, intelligent, intelligible and divine.

Gregory of Sinai
(1265-1346)

Archangel Michael
Russian Orthodox

he nature of our soul involves the will to command and exercise sovereignty, and that part by nature which serves and obeys. The will, desire, sensibility — all are powers of the soul. Since we have within us that which commands, God has granted us dominion over all the earth.

Gregory Palamas (1296-1359)

an is like another or second world—a new world, as he is called by Paul when he states, "Whoever is in Christ is a new creature" (2 Corinthians 5:17). For through virtue man becomes a heaven and an earth and everything that a world is.

Gregory of Sinai (1265-1346)

ll creatures are related to their Creator and depend upon Him. They may be referred to Him in three different ways: as He is the Principle who creates, the End who motivates, or the Gift who dwells within…. All creatures, however little they may partake of being, have God for their Principle; all rational beings, however little they may partake of light, are intended to grasp God through knowledge and love; and all righteous and holy souls possess the Holy Spirit as an infused gift.

Bonaventure (1221-1274)

The Virgin and Child
Fra Angelico

God made man according to His image and likeness. He deemed him worthy of the knowledge of Himself, that in preference to all of the animals He adorned him with rationality, bestowed upon him the opportunity of taking his delight in the unbelievable beauties of paradise, and made him the chief of the creatures on earth.

Basil the Great (329-379)

The virtue of innocence is held as foolishness by the wise of this world. Anything that is done out of innocence, they doubtless consider to be stupidity, and whatever truth approves of, in practice is called folly by men of worldly wisdom.

Gregory the Great (Pope) (540-604)

As long as one clings to time, space, number and quantity, that person is on the wrong track and God is strange and far away.... Those who relinquish their own wills completely will like what I teach and understand what I say. One authority has it that creatures receive their being directly from God, and that is why, in their true essence, creatures love God more than they love themselves.

Meister Eckhart (1260-1327)

e humble always and gentle, and patient too, putting up with one another's failings in a spirit of love.

Ephesians 4:2

This world and the world to come are two enemies. We cannot therefore be friends to both; but we must decide which we will forsake and which we will enjoy.

Pope Clement 1 (d. 101)

Spirituality is not to be learned by flight from the world, nor by running away from things, nor by turning solitary and going apart from the world. Rather we must learn an inner solitude wherever or with whomever we may be. We must learn to penetrate things and find God there.

Meister Eckhart (1260-1327)

Saint Dominic, detail from "The Mockery of Christ"
Fra Angelico

hen death comes, the mighty messenger of God, no king can command him, no authority can restrain him, no riches can hire him to wait past his appointed time even one moment of an hour. Therefore let us consider well in time what words we are bound to speak and what deeds we are bound to do, and let us say them and do them quickly. And let us leave unsaid and undone all superfluous things (and, much more, all damnable things), knowing well that we have no empty time allowed to us.

Thomas More (1477-1535)

hen we are sick, then we begin truly to know ourselves; then pain brings us home to ourselves; then we think how merry a thing it would be to pray in good health, though we can't do that now because of our grief…. Then we think within ourselves, that if ever we recover and mend in body, we will amend in soul, leave all vices, and be virtuously occupied for the rest of our life. For that reason, we should be, when we are healthy, as we think we would be when we are sick.

Thomas More (1477-1535)

Borgund Stave Church
Sogn, Norway

call it consolation when an interior movement is stirred up in the soul, by which it is set on fire with love of its Creator and Lord, and as a consequence can love no creature on the face of the earth for its own sake, but only in the Creator of them all. It is likewise consolation when we shed tears that move us to love God, whether it is because of sorrow for sins, or because of the sufferings of Christ our Lord, or for any other reason that is immediately directed to the praise and service of God. Finally, I call consolation every increase of faith, hope, and charity, and all interior joy that invites and attracts us to what is heavenly and to the salvation of our soul by filling it with peace and quiet in its Creator and Lord.

Ignatius of Loyola (1491-1556)

Medieval Illumination

Scenes from the life of Mary
Medieval Illumination

 on't imagine that, if you had a great deal of time, you would spend more of it in prayer. Get rid of that idea; it is no hindrance to prayer to spend your time well.

Teresa of Avila (1515-1582)

Madonna surrounded by Angels
Fra Angelico

he reason for loving God is God Himself; the measure of loving God is to love Him beyond measure.

Bernard of Clairvaux (1090-1153)

Let us remember, then, that within us there is a palace of immense magnificence. The entire edifice is built of gold and precious stones.... Truly there is no building of such great beauty as a pure soul, filled with virtues; and the greater these virtues, the brighter these stones sparkle.... In this palace the great King lodges, who has been pleased to become your Guest, and... He sits there on a throne of tremendous value: your heart.

Teresa of Avila (1515-1582)

Aspire to God with short but frequent outpourings of the heart; admire His bounty; invoke His aid; cast yourself in spirit at the foot of His cross; adore His goodness; treat with Him of your salvation; give Him your whole soul a thousand times in the day.

Francis de Sales (1567-1622)

look at how God dwells in the creatures, giving being to the elements, growth to the plants, sensation to animals, understanding to men.... I must consider how God works and labors for me in all things.... And then I must reflect upon myself.... I must look how all good things and gifts come down from above ... as justice, goodness, pity, mercy, etc., even as the rays of the light come from the sun and the waters from the spring.

Ignatius of Loyola (1491-1556)

t appears that the entire world is like a single mirror, full of lights that stand in the presence of the Divine Wisdom, shedding light like burning coals.

Bonaventure (1221-1274)

e, therefore, who is not illumined by such great splendor of created things, is blind; he who is not awakened by such great clamor is deaf; he who does not praise God because of all these effects is dumb; he who does not note the first principle from such great signs is foolish.

Open your eyes, therefore, prick up your spiritual ears, open your lips and apply your heart, that you may see, hear, praise, love and worship, glorify and honor your God.

Bonaventure (1221-1274)

The Last Judgment
Baptistery of San Giovanni, Florence
Byzantine

Whatever good or evil befalls you, be confident that God will convert it all to your good.

Jane Frances de Chantal (1572-1641)

Before going to bed make a general examination of conscience, then ... go to sleep with a good thought in your mind.

Vincent de Paul (1576-1660)

It is not always in the soul's power not to feel a temptation. But it is always in its power not to consent to it.

Francis de Sales (1567-1622)

Certain virtues are greatly esteemed and always preferred by the general run of men because they are close at hand, easily noticed, and in effect material. Thus many people prefer bodily to spiritual alms; hair shirts, fasting, going barefoot, using the discipline and physical mortifications to meekness, patience, modesty, and other mortifications of the heart ... although the latter are really higher virtues.

Francis de Sales (1567-1622)

Sainte Chapelle, Paris
High Gothic

Would you walk in earnest toward devotion? Seek some good man who will guide you; this is the greatest of all words of advice.

Francis de Sales (1567-1622)

Open your eyes, and behold, the whole world is full of God.

Jacob Boehme (1575-1624)

The Cathedral of Notre
Dame of Rheims
Gothic

God's majesty is present in all things, through His indwelling, through His works and through His essence, and can therefore be found in all things, in speaking, walking, seeing, tasting, hearing, thinking, and in whatever else we may do.

Ignatius of Loyola (1491-1556)

The whole outward visible world with all its being is a signature, or a figure of the inward spiritual world; whatever is internally, and however its operation is, so likewise it has its character externally; like as the spirit of each creature sets forth and manifests the internal form of its birth by its body, so does the Eternal Being also.

Jacob Boehme (1575-1624)

hen the Light of God first manifesteth itself in the soul, it shineth forth as light from a candle, and kindleth the outward light of reason immediately; yet it yieldeth not itself wholly up to reason, so as to be under the dominion of the outward man. No, the outward man beholdeth himself in this through-shining luster, as he doth his likeness in a looking-glass, whereby he presently learneth to know himself.

Jacob Boehme (1575-1624)

aradise is still in the world, but man is not in Paradise unless he is born again. Then he tastes here and now the eternal life for which he was made.

Jacob Boehme (1575-1624)

Celtic Door
Herefordshire, England

he Blessed Virgin, by becoming the mother of God, received a kind of infinite dignity because God is infinite; this dignity therefore is such a reality that a better one is not possible, just as nothing can be better than God.

Thomas Aquinas (1225-1274)

hat is the source of patience?
What is the source of faith, of hope, of charity?
The same compassion that gives birth to mercy.
What frees the soul from herself and binds her to You?
This compassion achieved in the light.
O lovely compassion achieved in the light.
O compassion,
you are a balm that snuffs out rage and cruelty in the soul.
This compassion, Compassionate Father,
I beg You to give to all creatures,
especially to those You have given me to love with a special love.

Catherine of Siena (1347-1380)

y creatures are pilgrim travelers in this life, created to reach Me,
their ultimate goal....
Who sees and experiences this revelation of My Name being
glorified and praised in every created thing?
The soul who has shed her body and come to Me, her final goal,
sees it clearly, and in her vision she knows the truth....
She sees this fully and truly in My holy ones, in this blessed spirit,
in all other creatures, and even in the devils.

Catherine of Siena (1347-1380)

The Annunciation
Fra Angelico

𝔐ercy is the fulfillment of justice, not its abolition.

Thomas Aquinas (1225-1274)

Abbey of Notre Dame de Fontgombault
Romanesque

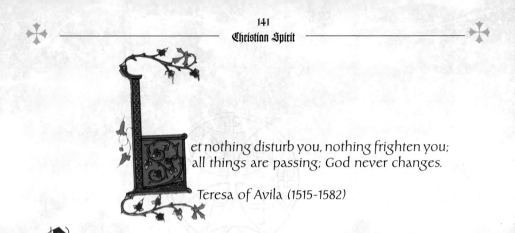

et nothing disturb you, nothing frighten you; all things are passing; God never changes.

Teresa of Avila (1515-1582)

Everything seems to me to pass so quickly ... that we must concentrate our thoughts on how to die rather than on how to live.

Teresa of Avila (1515-1582)

We know we have souls. But we seldom consider the precious things that can be found in this soul, or who dwells within it, or its high value. Consequently, little effort is made to preserve its beauty. All our attention is taken up with the plainness of the diamond's setting, that is, with these bodies of ours.

Teresa of Avila (1515-1582)

I knew well that I had a soul; but I did not understand the dignity of this soul, nor did I know who lodged within it, because my eyes were blinded by the vanities of this life, so that I was prevented from seeing Him. I think that, had I known then as I do now, that in this little palace of my soul so great a King is lodged, I would not have left Him alone so often, but at least sometimes I would have stayed with Him and been more careful to prepare a clean lodging for Him.

Teresa of Avila (1515-1582)

ivinity is the enfolding and unfolding of everything that is. Divinity is in all things in such a way that all things are in Divinity.

Nicholas of Cusa (1401-1464)

he true heaven is everywhere, even in that very place where thou standest and goest; and so when thy spirit presses through the astral and fleshly, and apprehends the inmost moving of God, then it is clearly in heaven.

Jacob Boehme (1575-1624)

h, how near is God to all things. Nevertheless, nothing can comprehend Him unless it be tranquil and surrenders to Him its own self-will. If this is accomplished, then will God be acting through the instrumentality of everything, like the sun that acts throughout the whole world.

Jacob Boehme (1575-1624)

his thou seest also in all God's works, how love hath poured itself into all things and is the most inward and outward foundation of all things…. That, O God, is Thy inward spiritual kingdom as Thou dwellest in that which is hidden and fillest all Thy creatures and workest Thyself and doest all in all….

The true heaven is everywhere in this present time until the last day, and the house of wrath, of hell and death, is also in this world, now, everywhere, until the last day…. Then will the earth, too, become crystalline, and the Divine Light will shine in all beings.

Jacob Boehme (1575-1624)

Enameled Bible cover
Limoges, France

Coronation of the Virgin
Medieval Illumination

In God alone is there primordial and true delight, and in all our delights it is this delight that we are seeking.

Bonaventure (1221-1274)

ou want us to serve You according to Your will, O Eternal Father, and You guide Your servants along different paths. And so today You show us that we neither may nor can in any way judge what is within a person by the actions we see.... Oh, how royally souls like this travel! In everything they see Your will, and so in everything which Your creatures do, they look for Your will, never passing judgment on any creature's intention.

Catherine of Siena (1347-1380)

hile observing that gaze [of God] never leaves anyone, one may see that It takes such diligent care of each one as though It cared only for him, and for no other, and this to such a degree that one on whom It rests cannot even conceive that It takes care of any other. One will also see that It takes the same most diligent care of the least of creatures as of the greatest, and of the whole universe.

Nicholas of Cusa (1401-1464)

reating and being created are one—yet this is no real difficulty, since with Thee creation and existence are the same. And creating and being created alike are naught else than the sharing of Thy Being among all, that Thou mayest be All in all, and yet mayest abide freed from all.

Nicholas of Cusa (1401-1464)

St. Francis of Assisi
preaching to the birds

My brothers, birds, you should praise your Creator very much and always love Him; He gave you feathers to clothe you, wings so that you could fly, and whatever else was necessary for you. God made you noble among His creatures, and He gave you a home in the purity of the air; though you neither sow nor reap, He nevertheless protects and governs you without any solicitude on your part.

Francis of Assisi (1182-1226)

O Most High, Almighty, Good Lord God,
To Thee belongs all praise, glory, honor and blessing!
Praised be my Lord God with all His creatures;
And especially our brother the sun, who brings us the day,
And who brings us the light;
Fair is he, and shining with a very great splendor;
O Lord, to us he signifies Thee!

Francis of Assisi (1182-1226)

Lord, make me an instrument of Your peace; where there is hatred, let me sow love; where there is injury, pardon; where there is doubt, faith; where there is despair, hope; where there is darkness, light; and where there is sadness, joy. O Divine Master, grant that I may not so much seek to be consoled as to console; to be understood as to understand; to be loved as to love; for it is in giving that we receive, it is in pardoning that we are pardoned, and it is in dying that we are born to eternal life.

Francis of Assisi (1182-1226)

Basilica of St. Francis, Assisi

ince God is the Universal Cause of all beings, in whatever region Being can be found, there must be the Divine Presence.

Thomas Aquinas (1225-1274)

e believe all things to have been made for man's sake, wherefore all things are stated to be subject to him. Now they serve man in two ways, first as sustenance of his bodily life, and secondly, as helping him to know God, inasmuch as man sees the invisible things of God by the things that are made.

Thomas Aquinas (1225-1274)

ime itself is contained within the universe, and therefore when we speak about creation, we should not inquire at what time it happened.... Creation precisely states a principle of origin, but not necessarily a principle of duration.... God is before the world in duration, yet the word before does not mean a priority of time, but of eternity perhaps, if you like, an endlessness of imaginary time.

Thomas Aquinas (1225-1274)

Detail from "The Last Judgment"
Fra Angelico

St. Francis' Tomb, Assisi

raised be my Lord for our sister, the death of the body,
    From whom no man escapeth.
Woe to him who dieth in mortal sin!
    Blessed are they who are found walking by Thy most holy will,
For the second death shall have no power to do them harm.
    Praise ye, and bless ye the Lord, and give thanks unto Him,
And serve Him with great humility.

Francis of Assisi (1182-1226)

No one is so foolish as not to believe that the things of the physical world are subject to someone's government, providence, and disposition, seeing that they are regulated according to a certain order and time. Thus we see the sun, the moon, and the stars and other parts of the physical world all holding a certain course, which would not happen if they were the sport of chance. For that reason, a man would be a fool not to believe in God.

Thomas Aquinas (1225-1274)

Church of Santo Spirito, Florence

Cross reliquary
Limburg

In this light my spirit suddenly saw through all; and in and by all the creatures, even in herbs and grass, it knew God, who He is and how He is and what His will is. And suddenly in that light my will was set on by a mighty impulse to describe the Being of God.

Jacob Boehme (1575-1624)

The greatest obstacle in the understanding of the doctrines in regard to divine mysteries is that the student imagines that they are dealing with things existing outside of himself and with which he is not concerned. But these doctrines are called "secret," not because they are not to be revealed, except to a few favorites, but because they cannot be understood unless the reader can free himself from that delusive conception of self which causes him to fancy that he is something separated from the rest of the world, not only in regard to his bodily form, but also in regard to his real foundations.

Jacob Boehme (1575-1624)

Sainte Chapelle, Paris
High Gothic

f things always went wrong, no one could endure it; if things always went well, everyone would become arrogant.

Bernard of Clairvaux (1090-1153)

he grace of contemplation is granted only in response to a longing and insistent desire.

Bernard of Clairvaux (1090-1153)

elieve one who has tried: You shall find a fuller satisfaction in the woods than in books. The trees and the rocks will teach you what you cannot hear from the masters.

Bernard of Clairvaux (1090-1153)

overty was not found in heaven. It is abounded on earth, but man did not know its value. The Son of God, therefore, treasured it and came down from heaven to choose it for Himself, to make it precious to us.

Bernard of Clairvaux (1090-1153)

hat is more against reason than to attempt, using reason, to transcend reason itself? And what is more against faith than to be unwilling to believe what reason cannot attain?

Bernard of Clairvaux (1090-1153)

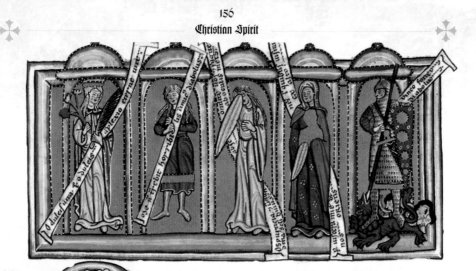

lants give off the fragrance of their flowers. The precious stones reflect their brilliance to others. Every creature yearns for a loving embrace. The whole of nature serves humanity, and in this service offers all her bounty.

Hildegard of Bingen (1098-1179)

he Creator loves His creation, so creation loves the Creator. Creation, of course, was fashioned to be adorned, to be gifted with the love of the Creator, and the entire world has been embraced by the kiss.

Hildegard of Bingen (1098-1179)

ithout the Word of God, no creature has meaning. God's Word is in all creation, visible and invisible. The Word is living, being, spirit, all verdant greening, all creativity. The Word manifests in every creature. Now this is how the Spirit is in the flesh — the Word is indivisible from God.

Hildegard of Bingen
(1098-1179)

nd again I heard the voice from heaven, saying to me: "The visible and the temporal is a manifestation of the invisible and the eternal."

Hildegard of Bingen
(1098-1179)

ll living creatures are, so to speak, sparks from the radiation of God's brilliance, and these sparks emerge from God likes the rays of the sun.

Hildegard of Bingen
(1098-1179)

Christ, Lord of the World
Hildegard of Bingen
Medieval Illumination

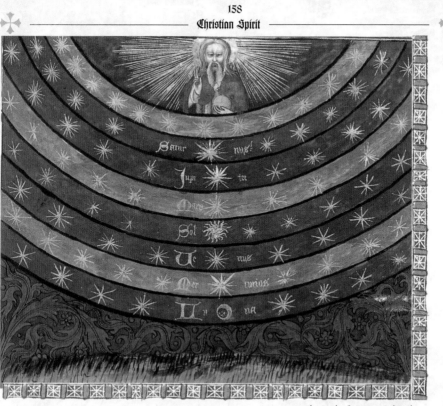

The Book of Heaven and Earth
Medieval French manuscript

or seeing the circling of heaven and the course of sun and moon, the positions and revolutions of the stars which are opposed and different, but in their difference all keep a common order, who would not think that they do not order themselves but that there is another Who orders and made them? And who, seeing the sun rise by day and the moon shining by night, waning and waxing unchangingly according to an exacting number of days, and some stars crossing and variously changing their paths while others keep a fixed place, who then would not consider that there must be a Creator Who governs them?

Athanasius (297-373)

ome people, in order to discover God, read books. But there is a great book: the very appearance of created things. Look above you! Look below you! Note it. Read it. God, Whom you want to discover, never wrote that book with ink. Instead He set before your eyes the things that He had made. Can you ask for a louder voice than that? Why, heaven and earth shout to you: "God made me!"

Augustine of Hippo (354-430)

Dante and Beatrice
Codex Urbinato

Etate illi uita / gaudete cum leticia qui
lem et conne / tristicia tustis ut eru iteris
mm faciatt / et faciemm ab ubribus
omnes qui diligitis eam / consolacionis uir. ps.

ll gifts of nature and grace have been given to us on loan. Their ownership is not ours, but always God's.

Meister Eckhart (1260-1327)

ou cannot know God by means of any creature science, nor by any means which relies upon your own wisdom....If you are to know God in His divinity, your own knowledge must become as pure ignorance, in which you forget yourself and every other creature.

Meister Eckhart (1260-1327)

ll that a man has here externally in multiplicity is intrinsically One. Here all blades of grass, wood and stone, all things are One. This is at their deepest depth.... If the soul knows God in creatures, night falls. If it sees how they have their being in God, morning breaks. But if it sees the Being that is in God himself alone, it is high noon! See! This is what one ought to desire with mad fervor, that all his life should become Being.

Meister Eckhart (1260-1327)

Bible Illumination
Medieval manuscript

Index of Author Quotations

For a glossary of all key foreign words used in books published by World Wisdom,
including metaphysical terms in English, consult:
www.DictionaryofSpiritualTerms.org.
This on-line Dictionary of Spiritual Terms provides extensive definitions,
examples and related terms in other languages.

Biographical Notes

MICHAEL AND JUDITH FITZGERALD have spent extended periods of time visiting traditional cultures and attending sacred ceremonies throughout the world. Michael Oren Fitzgerald has written and edited numerous publications on world religions, predominantly American Indian spirituality. He is a licensed attorney and holds a Doctor of Jurisprudence, cum laude, from Indiana University. Michael has taught Religious Traditions of the North American Indians in the Indiana University Continuing Studies Department in Bloomington, Indiana. Judith Fitzgerald is a graduate of Indiana University. She is an artisan, calligrapher, and graphic designer, and collaborated with Michael on the successful inspirational quote book, *Indian Spirit* (World Wisdom, 2003). They are married, have an adult son, and live in Bloomington, Indiana.

What others have said about
Michael Oren Fitzgerald

"(He) has a great sense of discernment in selecting editorial material which addresses directly the concerns of contemporary man."

—**Seyyed Hossein Nasr**, the George Washington University

"I greatly appreciate the recovery work that Fitzgerald is doing, work that makes available for the classroom and popular use texts that have been all but buried in libraries. Work such as Fitzgerald's is exactly the kind of work that needs to be promoted for a more complete understanding of early American Indian writings and oratory."

—**Stephen Brandon**, University of New Mexico

Free Christian e-Products

Daily Inspirational Quotations. Judith and Michael Fitzgerald have also selected several additional Christian inspirational quotations that were not used in *Christian Spirit* and designed and created many patterns of Christian e-stationery for use on the Internet. The quotations and e-stationery are combined to create "daily inspirational Christian quotations" that can be automatically sent to readers each day via e-mail at no charge. Interested readers should visit the e-Products section of the publisher's Internet site at:

www.worldwisdom.com

Other free e-Products

Judith Fitzgerald has also created Christian wallpaper, screen savers, e-cards, and e-stationery that are available for no cost at the same website. New products are periodically added.

World Wisdom provides all of these products to readers at no cost. The publisher and the editors hope these products will also provide a source of daily inspiration.